ALL ABOUT ARACHNIDS

BLACK WIDOWS

by Jenna Lee Gleisner

pogo

Ideas for Parents and Teachers

Pogo Books let children practice reading informational text while introducing them to nonfiction features such as headings, labels, sidebars, maps, and diagrams, as well as a table of contents, glossary, and index.

Carefully leveled text with a strong photo match offers early fluent readers the support they need to succeed.

Before Reading

- "Walk" through the book and point out the various nonfiction features. Ask the student what purpose each feature serves.
- Look at the glossary together. Read and discuss the words.

Read the Book

- Have the child read the book independently.
- Invite them to list questions that arise from reading.

After Reading

- Discuss the child's questions. Talk about how they might find answers to those questions.
- Prompt the child to think more. Ask: What did you know about black widows before reading this book? What more would you like to learn about this arachnid?

Pogo Books are published by Jump!
5357 Penn Avenue South
Minneapolis, MN 55419
www.jumplibrary.com

Copyright © 2025 Jump!
International copyright reserved in all countries.
No part of this book may be reproduced in any form without written permission from the publisher.

Library of Congress Cataloging-in-Publication Data

Names: Gleisner, Jenna Lee, author.
Title: Black widows / by Jenna Lee Gleisner.
Description: Minneapolis, MN: Jump!, Inc., [2025]
Series: All about arachnids | Includes index.
Audience: Ages 7-10
Identifiers: LCCN 2024037356 (print)
LCCN 2024037357 (ebook)
ISBN 9798892136099 (hardcover)
ISBN 9798892136105 (paperback)
ISBN 9798892136112 (ebook)
Subjects: LCSH: Black widow spider—Juvenile literature.
Classification: LCC QL458.42.T54 G54 2025 (print)
LCC QL458.42.T54 (ebook)
DDC 595.4/4—dc23/eng/20240903
LC record available at https://lccn.loc.gov/2024037356
LC ebook record available at https://lccn.loc.gov/2024037357

Editor: Katie Chanez
Designer: Emma Almgren-Bersie

Photo Credits: stphillips/iStock, cover, 1, 23; spxChrome/iStock, 3; Antagain/iStock, 4; Jay Ondreicka/Shutterstock, 5; Anton Sorokin/Alamy, 6-7, 18-19; lighTTrace Studio/Shutterstock, 8-9; Sari Oneal/Shutterstock, 10; James H. Robinson/Science Source, 11; samray/Shutterstock, 12-13; Brberrys/Shutterstock, 14; Sari O'Neal/Alamy, 15; EdwardSnow/iStock, 16-17; Ryan Walters/Alamy, 20-21.

Printed in the United States of America at Corporate Graphics in North Mankato, Minnesota.

TABLE OF CONTENTS

CHAPTER 1
Red Warning...4

CHAPTER 2
Brown Spiderlings......................................10

CHAPTER 3
Black Spinners...14

ACTIVITIES & TOOLS
Try This!...22
Glossary..23
Index..24
To Learn More..24

CHAPTER 1
RED WARNING

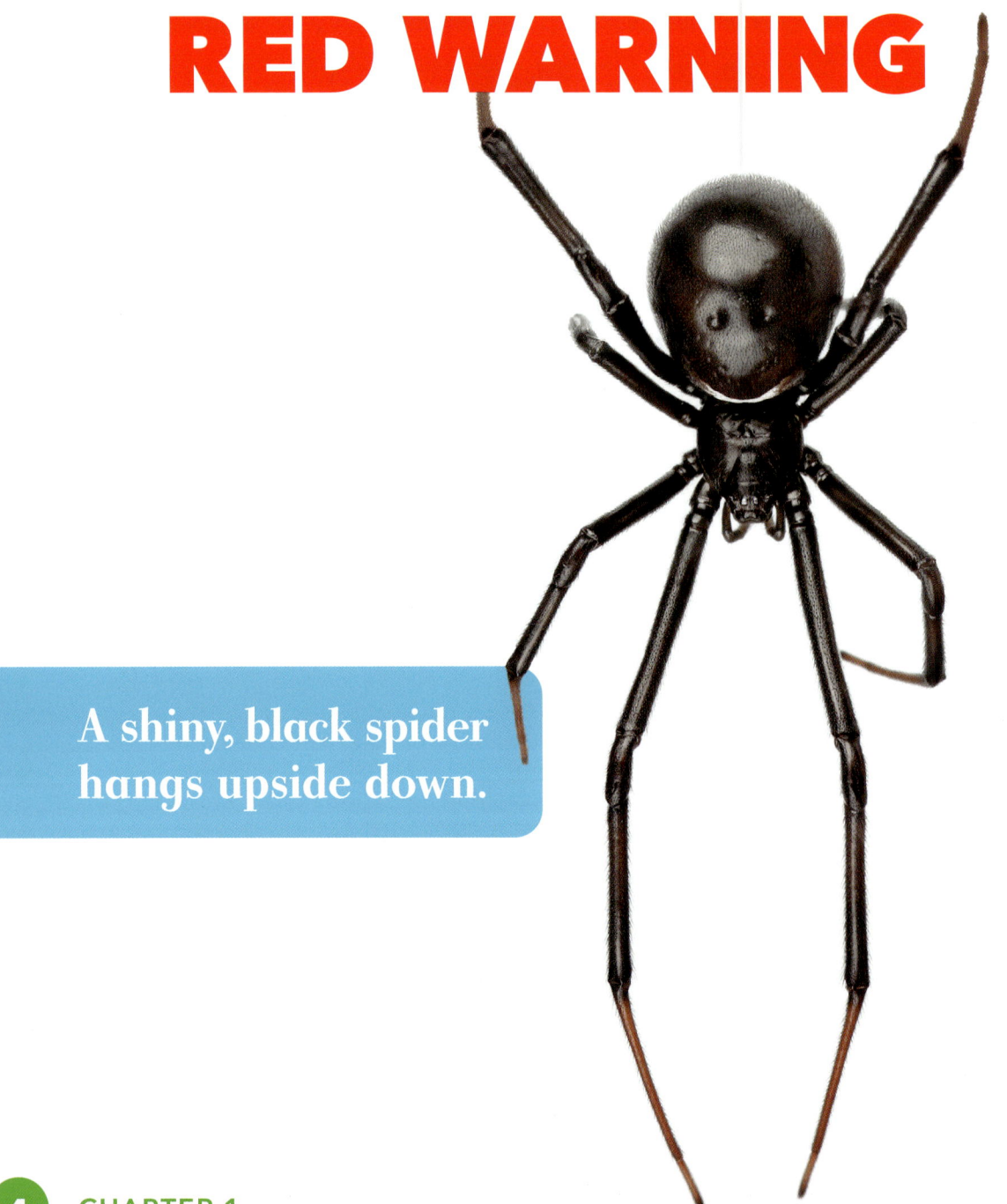

A shiny, black spider hangs upside down.

A red hourglass shape is on her belly. What is this **arachnid**? It is a black **widow**. The red is a warning. Stay away! This spider has **venom**.

hourglass shape

CHAPTER 1 | 5

Female black widows are black. Their bodies are round. They are about 1.5 inches (3.8 centimeters) long. Male black widows are half that size. They have long legs. They are gray or brown. They can have red or white marks.

male

TAKE A LOOK!

What are the parts of a female and male black widow? Take a look!

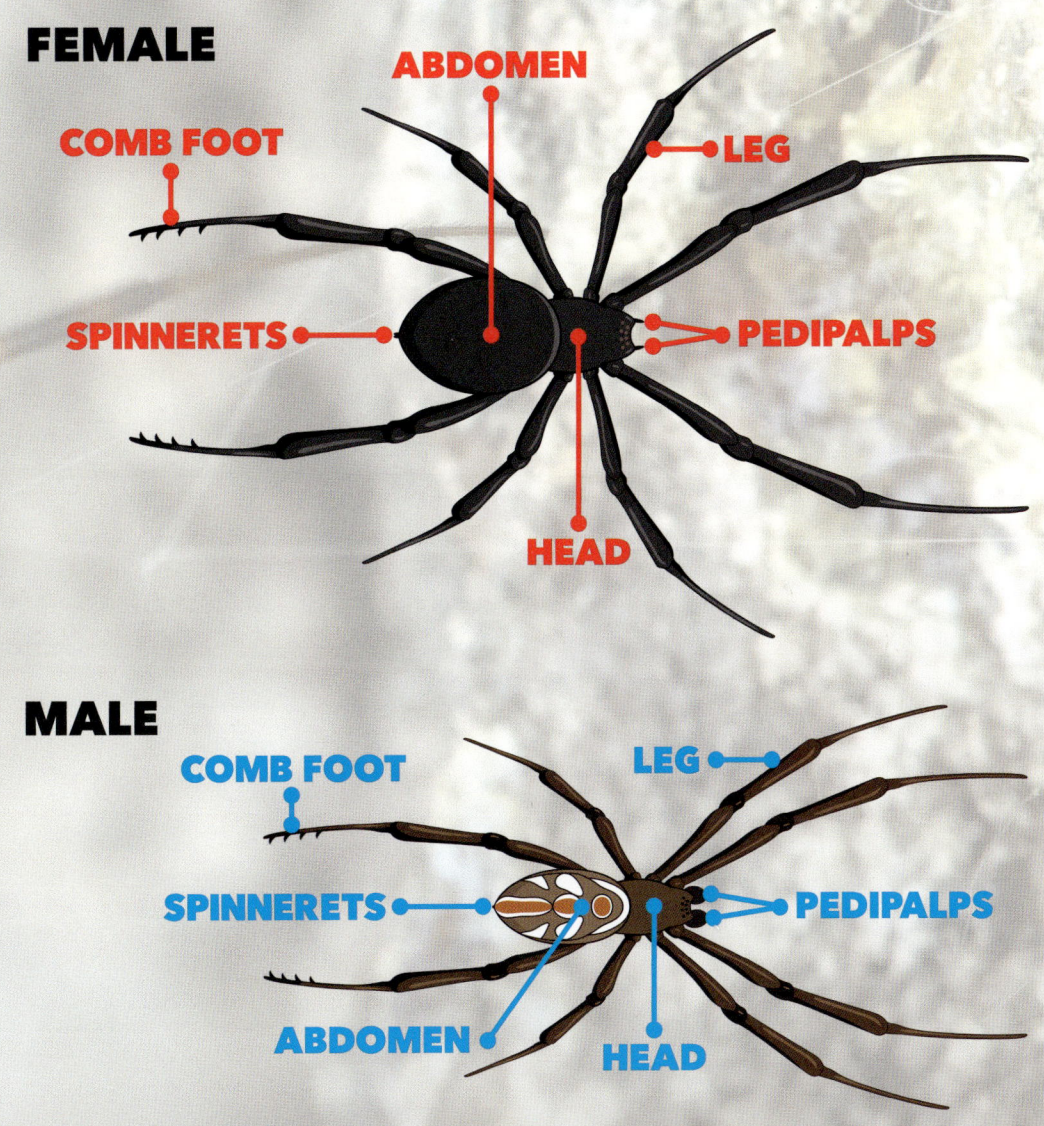

Males and females **mate**. How did the black widow get its name? A female will sometimes eat the male after mating. Her body uses the **nutrients** for her eggs.

DID YOU KNOW?

Females don't eat the males every time. Most of the time, the males get away.

CHAPTER 1

CHAPTER 2
BROWN SPIDERLINGS

An adult female makes many egg sacs. She spins the sacs with her silk. The sacs are white, tan, or gray. She puts her eggs in them. Hundreds of eggs are in each one! She protects them.

egg sacs

The **spiderlings** hatch. They are orange, white, or brown. Some eat each other.

spiderling

egg

CHAPTER 2

The rest leave the web. How? They **balloon**. They release silk. It attaches to something. Then the wind carries them away.

CHAPTER 2

CHAPTER 3
BLACK SPINNERS

After they balloon, the spiders build their own webs. They spin them with silk. Then they wait for **prey**.

Black widows cannot see well. But they feel. A bug touches her web. She quickly jumps on it.

Then she starts spinning! Using her comb foot, she wraps her prey in silk. It cannot get away. She bites it. Venom **paralyzes** the prey. Its insides turn to liquid. She sucks it up. *Slurp*!

DID YOU KNOW?

Black widows mostly eat **arthropods**. These include ants, beetles, and scorpions. Their shells are left behind after the black widow eats their insides.

CHAPTER 3

Black widows live around the world. Five **species** live in the United States. They live in forests, deserts, and **grasslands**. Some have red spots.

CHAPTER 3

Black widows are one of the most dangerous spiders in the United States. Their messy webs are often low, near the ground. It is best to leave these black spiders be!

DID YOU KNOW?

A black widow's venom is strong. Some say it is 15 times stronger than a rattlesnake's!

ACTIVITIES & TOOLS

TRY THIS!

RED WARNINGS

Black widows have red marks. In the animal kingdom, this is a sign they are venomous. What other red or bright colored animals can you think of? Research and compare with this fun activity!

What You Need:
- tablet or other device for researching
- pencil
- paper

1. Search online to find other animals that have red or other bright colors, such as yellow or blue.
2. Make a list of the animals you find. What bright color(s) do they have? Note their color as well.
3. Where do these animals live? What do their colors mean?
4. Compare your research to black widows. How many have red? Does it always mean they have venom?

GLOSSARY

arachnid: A creature with a body divided into two parts, such as a spider or a scorpion.

arthropods: Animals without a backbone that have a hard outer skeleton and three or more pairs of legs, such as insects, spiders, and lobsters.

balloon: To release silk for air to catch.

grasslands: Large, open areas of grass.

mate: To come together to produce babies.

nutrients: Substances that animals need to stay strong and healthy.

paralyzes: Makes something unable to move.

prey: Animals hunted by other animals for food.

species: One of the groups into which similar animals and plants are divided.

spiderlings: Baby spiders.

venom: Poison.

widow: A woman whose husband has died.

INDEX

balloon 13, 14
eat 8, 11, 16
eggs 8, 10
egg sacs 10
feel 15
female 6, 7, 8, 10
male 6, 7, 8
marks 6
mate 8
nutrients 8
paralyzes 16
prey 14, 16
silk 10, 13, 14, 16
size 6
species 19
spiderlings 11
spins 10, 14, 16
spots 19
venom 5, 16, 20
web 13, 14, 15, 20

TO LEARN MORE

Finding more information is as easy as 1, 2, 3.
❶ Go to www.factsurfer.com
❷ Enter "blackwidows" into the search box.
❸ Choose your book to see a list of websites.